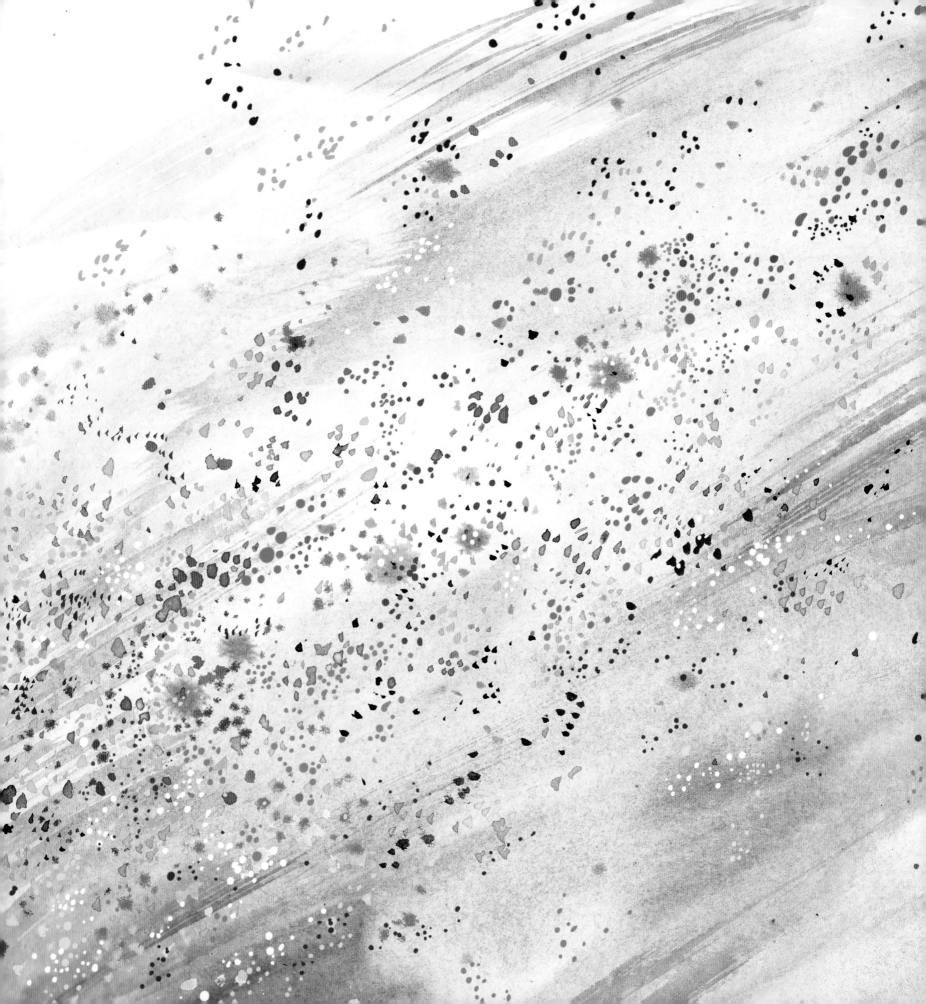

We Are a GARDEN

A STORY OF HOW DIVERSITY TOOK ROOT IN AMERICA

by LISA WESTBERG PETERS

illustrated by VICTORIA TENTLER-KRYLOV

schwartz & wade books · new york

Long ago a strong wind blew. It blew people, like seeds, to a new land.

It blew in a girl and her clan when glaciers still covered the north and herds of mammoths still wandered the frozen tundra. They walked across a wide plain and became the first people to live on the sprawling continent.

After countless summers and countless winters,
most of the glaciers had melted and the wide plain had
vanished beneath the sea. But the wind still blew. It blew
a boy and his family across the frigid waters in a canoe. They
camped on the shore and stayed to hunt bowhead whales.

For a long time, the wind was calm. Bison herds darkened the prairies and snowfall softened the mountains. The first people spread quickly across the new land. They hunted game in its forests, planted corn in its valleys, and built villages on its coasts, and the continent became home.

Then, much later, the wind began to blow again. It blew in newcomers from all directions. Some came peacefully, and others pushed aside or clashed with the people who had called the land home for longer than anyone could remember.

From the north, the wind blew those who lived in the forests
to a new home in the canyons and mesas of the desert.

From the south, the wind blew in a string of wagons carrying colonists through a land of mesquite bushes and across a wide river. They settled on a high desert plateau. But not long after, their brutal leader slaughtered the tribe that was living there.

From the east, it blew in a sailing ship carrying boys and men who hoped to find their fortune in gold and silver. Instead, they found hunting grounds and villages filled with families. When they had trouble growing their own food, they took the food supplies of the villagers.

The wind blew in slave ship after slave ship full of men, women, and children. Traders had forced them from their homes and across the ocean to work from sunup to sundown in the plantation fields, for people who did not treat them like humans.

And it blew in ships carrying families who were weary of hunger
in their homeland or longing to practice their religion freely.

21

From the west, the wind blew in steamships carrying poor farmers who came to lay miles and miles of railroad track. For very low wages, they worked on the steepest mountain passes and in the deepest ravines, and many lost their lives.

Later, the wind blew in millions of men, women, and children from the south to do the backbreaking work of harvesting the nation's crops—its cotton and rice, its lettuce and sugar beets.

As more and more people settled the land, the nation erected a
monument in its busiest port, welcoming everyone with these words:

> Give me your tired, your poor,
>
> Your huddled masses yearning to breathe free,
>
> The wretched refuse of your teeming shore.
>
> Send these, the homeless, tempest-tossed to me,
>
> I lift my lamp beside the golden door!

The wind still blows. It blows in . . .

27

. . . a baby who sleeps while her mother cleans hotel
rooms from dawn to dusk . . .

. . . and a grandmother who once escaped war in a rickety boat and now seeks shelter with her neighbors when a hurricane strikes the coast.

The wind blows in a thirteen-year-old refugee who adjusts her head scarf in the bright afternoon sun and declares she will be a doctor someday . . .

. . . and a fourth-grade boy who plays the same soccer
in his new home that he played in his first home.

Some people leave rocky soil and hard times behind
in their homelands.

Others find rocky soil and hard times in the new land.

But people, like seeds, take root.

Their roots form a tangled web,

their branches form a delicate filigree,

and their memories—some painful, some proud—

and their enduring hopes for the future linger and

mingle in the air.

"They" become "we," and we become a garden.
A garden of friends, family, and neighbors. A garden
of Americans who turn to face the wind.

37

GLOSSARY

ancestor: A family member who lived a long time ago.

descendant: Someone who is related to a person who lived in the past.

emigrate: To leave your native country to live permanently in another.

immigrate: To arrive in a foreign country to live permanently.

Indigenous (in-DIJ-i-nous) people: The first—the original—residents of an area. American Indians are the first residents of the land that became the United States. They lived here for thousands of years before other people did.

migrant: A person who migrates.

migrate: To move from one area or country to another.

A NOTE ABOUT THIS STORY

All Americans are migrants, the descendants of recent migrants, or the descendants of ancient migrants. Over the years, we have arrived by foot, boats made of animal skins, horseback, ship, car, plane, even bicycle. We have brought with us stone tools, weapons, deadly viruses, recipes, plants, toys, and mobile phones. Many things have pushed or pulled us to come, from the horror of war to simple curiosity about trying a new life. The migrants featured in this book are only some of the many groups who have made the United States their home. I chose them for many reasons, such as: they were the first to arrive, they came in great numbers, or they made significant agricultural or industrial contributions to our nation.

Pages 4–5, 6–7: The First People

Scientists are still investigating the details of when, how, and why we first came to the Americas. We know that several waves of people started migrating from northern Asia to Alaska more than fifteen thousand years ago, becoming the ancient ancestors of most of the Indigenous people of North and South America. The migrants then walked south and east across the two continents and probably used boats to travel along the western coastline. Scientists have learned about these long-ago migrations from the campsites the first people left behind and the genetic similarities between Indigenous people and Asians. Many American Indians today accept this migration story, but others do not because it conflicts with their traditional origin stories.

Pages 8–9: Arctic People

Between one and two thousand years ago, another group of people crossed from northern Asia to Alaska by boat, but this group did not migrate south. They stayed in the Arctic and became the ancestors of those who still live in the far northern regions of Alaska, Canada, and Greenland. In Alaska, their descendants are known today as the Iñupiat, Yup'ik, and Cup'ik. In Canada, they are known as the Inuit. Whale hunting is still part of their culture.

Pages 10–11, 12–13: Apache and Navajo Ancestors

The original residents of the land spent thousands of years here, establishing diverse cultures and adapting to many environments. It wasn't until about five hundred years ago that newcomers started arriving. People living in the forests of western Canada moved over a thousand miles to the desert Southwest and the plains, perhaps to follow herds of animals for hunting. We know this because the Apache and Navajo living in the Southwest today speak languages similar to those still spoken in western Canada; they are the descendants of the long-ago migrants. Today, large Apache and Navajo communities live in several states, including New Mexico, Arizona, Texas, and Oklahoma.

Pages 14–15: Spanish

The first Europeans to settle in the United States arrived in the 1500s from Spain. Many came to search for gold and silver, others to convert the people who already lived here to the Roman Catholic faith. In 1598, Spanish explorer Juan de Oñate led a group of colonists into New Mexico from northern Mexico and founded the town of Santa Fe. While exploring the territory, Oñate's soldiers demanded food from the Acoma people, who barely had enough for themselves. Angry and threatened, the Acoma attacked and killed several Spanish soldiers. Oñate wanted revenge, and a few months later, his soldiers killed several hundred Acoma people. The Spanish government soon convicted Oñate of using too much force to claim territory and control, and it ordered him back to Spain. He was never imprisoned for his crimes. In spite of all the early conflicts, both Spanish and indigenous influences have endured in the Southwest.

Pages 16–17: British

The British also wanted to find riches in the Americas. In 1606, the Virginia Company of London sent a small group of colonists across the Atlantic Ocean. They did not find gold or silver, and life in the colony they named Jamestown proved hard. The colonists couldn't grow enough corn, so they demanded corn from a group of tribes led by Chief Powhatan. In spite of the gifts of corn, many colonists died in their first year. Later the Powhatan Indians attacked the settlement because the British kept encroaching on Powhatan land. But Britain sent more colonists and supplies and the settlement survived.

Pages 18–19: Enslaved Africans

One of the worst examples of forced migration in history is the kidnapping and transport of millions of African villagers and farmers to the Americas to work on plantations. Slave ships from many countries—Portugal, Britain, France, Spain, and the Netherlands—crossed the Atlantic from the 1500s to the 1800s. The captured Africans endured unspeakable conditions, and many died on board the ships or after they arrived in the new land. President Lincoln freed America's enslaved people in 1863. Today African Americans make up about 14 percent of the US population.

Pages 20–21: Europeans

Millions of Europeans, especially Germans and Irish, immigrated here in the 1800s. They left Europe for many reasons, including hunger, lack of jobs, political unrest, and the inability to freely practice their religion. Many Germans found jobs digging canals, building railroads, and working as shoemakers and butchers. Half of all Irish people left their homeland, driven out by famine. (Potatoes were an important part of the Irish diet, and the potato crops had failed for several years.) Many Irish women became domestic workers, and like the Germans, many Irish men helped build industrial America.

Pages 22–23: Chinese

Chinese farmers began arriving on the West Coast in the mid-1800s. At first, they came to mine for gold in the mountains; later, they came to help build the nation's first transcontinental railroads. Even though the Chinese people were highly successful at the work they did on the railroads, they were paid less than white Americans and European immigrants. In the 1870s, as more Chinese arrived and economic hard times hit, resentment of the immigrants became widespread and Americans launched violent and racist anti-Chinese attacks. In 1882, the federal government finally passed a law forbidding Chinese immigration. The law remained in effect for sixty years.

Pages 24–25: Mexicans

In the early 1940s, many Americans were called away to serve in World War II. This created a shortage of workers at home, so the government signed agreements with Mexico allowing Mexicans to come here to harvest the crops and maintain railroads. Called the *bracero* ("laborer" in Spanish) program, it allowed millions to cross the border legally and receive higher wages than they could get in Mexico. But American growers and the railroad companies often mistreated the temporary workers, withholding their full pay or providing substandard housing.

Pages 26–27: The Statue of Liberty

In the late 1800s, France gave the Statue of Liberty to the United States to honor the freeing of enslaved people during the Civil War. Immigrants entering New York harbor in 1886 were the first to see this inspiring statue. Over time, the statue came to symbolize a welcoming embrace of immigrants to our country. New York writer Emma Lazarus helped bring about this shift when she wrote a poem, later sold at auction to raise money for the statue's base. Her poem welcomed all to our country and was engraved in its base in 1903.

Pages 28–37: Contemporary Immigration

Today more than one out of eight Americans (including a member of my own family) were born in another country. The greatest numbers of immigrants come from China, India, and Mexico, but they also come from just about every country in the world. They perform a wide variety of jobs, from physician to housekeeper, construction worker to software engineer. Immigrants are still arriving, and for many of the same reasons they always have.

Contemporary immigrants whose lives have crossed with mine helped inspire *We Are a Garden*. War became much more personal to me when I talked to Hmong schoolchildren about their horrific escape from it. I finally understood the meaning of the word "perseverance" when I helped Somali refugees write college papers as they juggled work, family, and school. And I've seen that the adjustment to American life can require a fair amount of grace and patience. When my kindergarten-aged granddaughter corrected her immigrant father's English, I was always surprised that he showed no irritation or frustration. Just pride.

SOURCES

I used many sources of information in researching *We Are a Garden*. Here are a few of them:

Center for History and New Media: Bracero History Archive
braceroarchive.org/about

The Colonial Williamsburg Foundation and UNESCO's Slave Route Project, "Slavery and Remembrance"
slaveryandremembrance.org/articles/article/?id=A0032

Inuit Circumpolar Council Alaska iccalaska.org/icc-alaska

Library of Congress: A Journey in Chains
loc.gov/teachers/classroommaterials/presentationsandactivities /presentations/immigration/african3.html

National Park Service: A Legacy from the Far East
nps.gov/gosp/learn/historyculture/a-legacy-from-the-far-east.htm

National Park Service: America, the Nation of Nations
nps.gov/articles/nationofnations.htm

National Park Service: Jamestown, A place of Many Beginnings
hnps.gov/jame/index.htm

National Park Service: Push and Pull Factors
nps.gov/teachers/classrooms/push-and-pull-factors.htm

Navajopeople.org: Ancient Navajo and Native Americans Migrations
navajopeople.org/blog/ancient-navajo-and-native-americas-migrations

New Mexico History: Juan de Oñate
newmexicohistory.org/2013/01/10/juan-de-onate/

New York Times: "Crossing From Asia, the First Americans Rushed Into the Unknown" nytimes.com/2018/11/08/science/prehistoric-migration-americas.html

Pew Research Center: Key findings about U.S. immigrants
pewresearch.org/fact-tank/2018/11/30/key-findings-about-u-s-immigrants/

The Statue of Liberty–Ellis Island Foundation, Inc.: Immigration Timeline
libertyellisfoundation.org/immigration-timeline

For Ingrid, Alba, and Julia, my favorite descendants of migrants —L.W.P.

*To my family, who came to the United States to start a new life,
and to the United States, which I love like no other country in the world* —V.T.-K.

ACKNOWLEDGMENTS

For their help in answering questions along the way, I thank William Fitzhugh of the Smithsonian Institution's Arctic Studies Center; Eske Willerslev of the Lundbeck Foundation GeoGenetics Centre at the University of Copenhagen; Mary Linn of the Smithsonian Center for Folklife and Cultural Heritage; and Nicole Martin Rogers, White Earth Nation descendant. For invaluable advice and suggestions, I thank my agent, Sue Cohen, and writing colleagues Susan Marie Swanson, Lindsay Johnson, Rick Chrustowski, and Lauren Stringer. For their endless patience and dedication to this book, thanks to my editor, Anne Schwartz, and her assistant, Anne-Marie Varga. For inspiration a long time ago, thanks to a group of fourth and fifth graders at Mississippi Creative Arts School in St. Paul, Minnesota. And a final thanks to my daughters, to their families, and to my husband, Dave, for steady companionship and support.—L.W.P.

Visit us on the Web! rhcbooks.com
Educators and librarians, for a variety of teaching tools, visit us at RHTeachersLibrarians.com

Library of Congress Cataloging-in-Publication Data is available upon request.
ISBN 978-0-593-12313-3 (hc) — ISBN 978-0-593-12314-0 (lib. bdg.) — ISBN 978-0-593-12315-7 (ebook)

The text of this book is set in ITC Novarese 13-point type.
The illustrations were rendered in watercolor and finished digitally in Adobe Photoshop.
Book design by Rachael Cole

MANUFACTURED IN CHINA
1 3 5 7 9 10 8 6 4 2
First Edition

Random House Children's Books supports the First Amendment and celebrates the right to read.